A DEDICATION

To our children,

to generations not yet born, and

to the planet that sustains us all.

We honor and acknowledge people all over the world, past and present, doing work that will move us toward *a world that works for all.*

Amazement. Awe. Astonishment.
To Ponder. Muse. Get curious.
Wonderment. Wonder-full.

Could wonder be an antidote to moral judgments?
Have we lost our sense of wonder as adults?
Is wondering a pillar of love and care?

Wonder opens us up.
Like walking through the cacophony of color and scent of a rose garden in Spring.
Or gazing into the eyes of an infant. *The eternal wondering.*
We blossom with *wonder.*

Wonder is a doorway to Interconnectivity.
To pause. To contemplate.

Wonder invites curiosity and amazement to rise because it's an open door policy.
Nothing is too giant, or too teeny, *to wonder about.*

Wonder is an invitation to wisdom and astonishment.

Wonder holds hands with not-knowing. Living into questions. Letting our hearts rise.
It allows answers to come from sifting and winnowing. From an insatiable curiosity.
We become.

Wonder breathes life into the deep forgotten nests of childhood, for some.
Emanating from the very essence of our beingness.

Wonder is inside us. And all around.
The wind whispers it.
The grasses sway because of it.
It's a practice. An art. A dance. A skill.
A wellspring of nourishment.
Available for you to receive any time, my friends.

Let's raise the voice of wonder up together. *Join us.*

A workbook to
explore consciousness
and reshape culture

CAROL DELMONICO & CASEY DAVIS

ARTWORK BY KAREN RUANE

CREATED BY AND FOR

the curious, the courageous, & the broken-hearted.

Conceived on a smoke-filled day in Central Oregon, the workbook's fifty-two questions rained down seemingly in an instant. In truth, they were born of years of wondering about the fate of humanity in a culture that has seemingly lost its way. As a society we've grown ill, forgetting the power of connection and care for each other and the earth, locked up in private lives and spaces. The collective 'we' has been replaced by the individualistic 'me'.

This project is a *wake up call.*

Its aim is to set a million small fires in the consciousness of many, urging us to snap out of the trance and begin to act on behalf of more than our small selves.

Wonder upRising is where mindfulness meets social and environmental well-being. It urges us to pull out our equity lens, clean it off and get to work. Now more than ever, the world needs all of us to grow into and offer our highest qualities in service to creating a world that works for all. Like a skilled teacher or wise elder, the workbook does not give us the answers. It asks the questions that need our attention, provides writing prompts that move us along on our journey, and clarifies our part in creating a more equitable world. Along the way, we identify our biases, blindspots, and passions, and take action in our own way. In this process of deep, honest reflection, we are changing our brains, shifting our habits and becoming the change we wish to see.

Powerful and transformative when done alone, the workbook is an equally dynamic resource for small groups. It's a community builder, a grower of equity muscles, and a practice that helps us see through a wider and deeper lens. It calls us to think with our hearts and minds. Our suggested facilitation guide is based on equitable sharing, ensuring all voices are heard, and a *'listening only'* process that provides space for everyone to be acknowledged and seen. It's also an opportunity to listen to our own internal narratives as we hear others. It's about turning to wonder instead of reacting in judgment when discomfort arises.

Since the spring of 2018, we've been piloting the process in schools, our local library, spiritual centers, common spaces and living rooms. We've watched people walk in as strangers and walk away friends. We've seen people find their voice and share their truth. Some have vowed to change their wills to better reflect their values. Some have committed to shift their daily habits and model a different way of being for their children. We've seen all sizes and shapes of consciousness shifting. We are grateful to witness the transformation that occurs in and between each of us. We are on this journey together.

We are two passionate and compassionate women who care deeply about humankind and the more than human world. ***This project is our commitment to heal both for our children, our communities and for future generations.***

Carol + Casey

Why WRITE?

Writing allows us to access the parts of ourselves hidden down deep. Guided by questions and prompts filled with wonder and exploration, we are led to limitless possibilities and potentials unknown.

Writing turns our thoughts into words that our eyes can see. And when spoken, we can hear ourselves and see others in new ways.

Why SHARE?

Sharing this process with others amplifies our connectivity. We are changed when we connect deeply and authentically. The biology of being seen, heard and witnessed changes us as we glimpse the depths we share.

These moments are like gems of hope. They are based in listening and understanding, not always liking and agreeing. We are rewiring in community.

We are opening new neuropathways of cooperation, collaboration and care.

How to use this Workbook:

Each page is a journey. Each question is laid out as a two-page spread. The top left corner is where it begins, with the primary evocative question.

The prompts are sprinkled across the pages. Answer them in any order that pleases you. Dive into the prompts that resonate and skip the ones that don't.

Save "*What's Rising Up?*", on the bottom of the second page, for the end of your journey. What has become clear? Is there an action you want to take? A behavior you want to look at more closely? What is the part you want to play now?

Ways to use it:

- **Self Study:** Do it on your own.
- **The Buddy System:** Find a partner and share.
- **Bridge the Divide:** Reconnect with family members or friends who are far away in location or perspective.
- **Groups:** Bring this workbook to already established groups: congregations, schools, work groups, board rooms, trainings, spiritual communities, or start a group in your living room.

(For guidance with groups, see pgs. 134 & 135.)

Table of Contents

- 9   Self-Awareness
- 21   Cultural Norms
- 33   We the People
- 45   The More than Human World
- 61   Legacy
- 73   Belonging
- 85   Community
- 97   Inclusivity
- 109   Connectivity
- 121   Compassion

RESOURCES

- 132   Four Windows of Wonder
- 132   Sensations List
- 133   Feelings List
- 134   Facilitation Guide
- 135   Group Process Guide

ARE YOU SEARCHING FOR
THE CURRENT INSIDE YOU?

THE ONE THAT RUNS
UNDERWATER.

THE MYSTERIOUS,
SUBMERGED PARTS
OF YOURSELF.

THEY ARE
THERE
WAITING
FOR YOU.

Self-Awareness

Knowing ourselves is knowing others.

And knowing others is knowing ourselves.
We are mirrors.
Self-awareness is an inward and outward reflection.
It's part of our adolescent stage that often isn't done in adolescence. Or you could call it our second adulthood.

Do we have to develop the self to be a non-self?

Do we need self-awareness in order to be aware of the greater world we inhabit?

We can be differentiated, self-aware and
inextricably interconnected.
I don't "think" therefore I am.
I feel, I sense, I imagine *and* think therefore I am.
Self-awareness leads us through and towards
deeper windows of wonder.

Inclusive of self and other.

WHAT DOES YOUR
Soul want to say
TO THE WORLD?

I wonder and question...

Initial **thoughts & feelings** / One minute **rant**

What can we **carry forward** from the past?
What can we **leave behind?**

How do our **great-great-grandchildren**
hope we answer this question?

I wonder what the **dominant culture** is telling me?

What is the part of this **I don't want to talk about?**
What are the stories I am telling myself?

What does your **heart** want?

HOW TO BE?

WHAT TO DO?

WHAT'S RISING UP?

WHAT TO HAVE/KNOW?

WHAT TO IMAGINE...

This week, I intend to:

HOW HAS **PAIN BEEN A TEACHER** FOR YOU?

I wonder and question...

Initial **thoughts & feelings** / One minute **rant**

What can we **carry forward** from the past?
What can we **leave behind?**

How do our **great-great-grandchildren**
hope we answer this question?

I wonder what the **dominant culture** is telling me?

What is the part of this **I don't want to talk about?**
What are the stories I am telling myself?

What does your **heart** want?

HOW TO BE?

WHAT TO DO?

WHAT'S RISING UP?

WHAT TO HAVE/KNOW?

WHAT TO IMAGINE...

This week, I intend to:

WHAT ARE YOUR SUPER POWERS?

Don't know? Ask five people to name your top three qualities and see if there are patterns.

I wonder and question...

Initial **thoughts & feelings** / One minute **rant**

What can we **carry forward** from the past?
What can we **leave behind**?

How do our **great-great-grandchildren**
hope we answer this question?

I wonder what the **dominant culture** is telling me?

What is the part of this **I don't want to talk about?**
What are the stories I am telling myself?

What does your **heart** want?

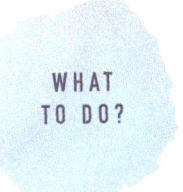 HOW TO BE?

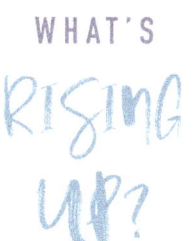 WHAT TO DO?

WHAT'S RISING UP?

 WHAT TO HAVE/KNOW?

 WHAT TO IMAGINE...

This week, I intend to:

WHAT ARE THE TOP 5 WAYS YOU DISCONNECT FROM YOUR FEELINGS AND INTIMATE RELATIONSHIPS?

I wonder and question...

Initial **thoughts & feelings** / One minute **rant**

What can we **carry forward** from the past?
What can we **leave behind?**

How do our **great-great-grandchildren**
hope we answer this question?

I wonder what the **dominant culture** is telling me?

What is the part of this **I don't want to talk about?**
What are the stories I am telling myself?

What does your **heart** want?

HOW TO BE?

WHAT TO DO?

WHAT'S RISING UP?

WHAT TO HAVE/KNOW?

WHAT TO IMAGINE...

This week, I intend to:

WHAT DOES SUCCESS MEAN TO YOU?

Could you shift the definition to include more caring and sharing?

Write about that.

I wonder and question...

Initial **thoughts & feelings** / One minute **rant**

What can we **carry forward** from the past?
What can we **leave behind**?

How do our **great-great-grandchildren**
hope we answer this question?

I wonder what the **dominant culture** is telling me?

What is the part of this **I don't want to talk about?**
What are the stories I am telling myself?

What does your **heart** want?

HOW TO BE?

WHAT TO DO?

WHAT'S RISING UP?

WHAT TO HAVE/KNOW?

WHAT TO IMAGINE...

This week, I intend to:

We are shaped by the world around us, and we shape it.

It takes wisdom and courage to let go of what doesn't serve us.

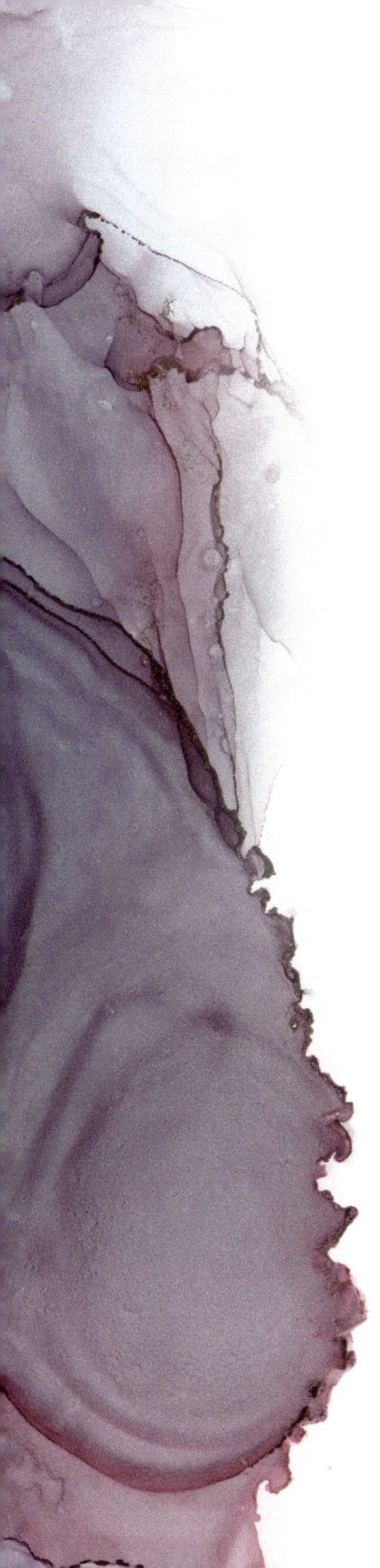

Cultural Norms

These are the daily habits that are lived by the majority of people in a place. Business as usual.

Of word, of deed,
of what and where and why you consume.
Of what you eat.
How we treat each other.

Both our collective consciousness
and our collective disconnection.
This is the ground that is recreated, changeable.
Choice.

Driving a car is a norm in our culture,
living in separate spaces is a norm for many,
grocery stores teeming with food products is a norm,
flushing toilets with potable water is a norm,
community as two is a norm.

HOW DOES BEING CALLED *a consumer* AFFECT YOUR THINKING, FEELING, AND BUYING PRACTICES?

What would change if you were called
- *and believed yourself to be* -
a citizen first and foremost?

I wonder and question...

Initial **thoughts & feelings** / One minute **rant**

What can we **carry forward** from the past?
What can we **leave behind**?

How do our **great-great-grandchildren**
hope we answer this question?

I wonder what the **dominant culture** is telling me?

What is the part of this **I don't want to talk about?**
What are the stories I am telling myself?

What does your **heart** want?

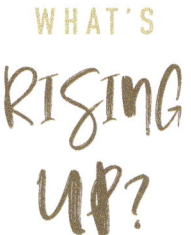

This week, I intend to:

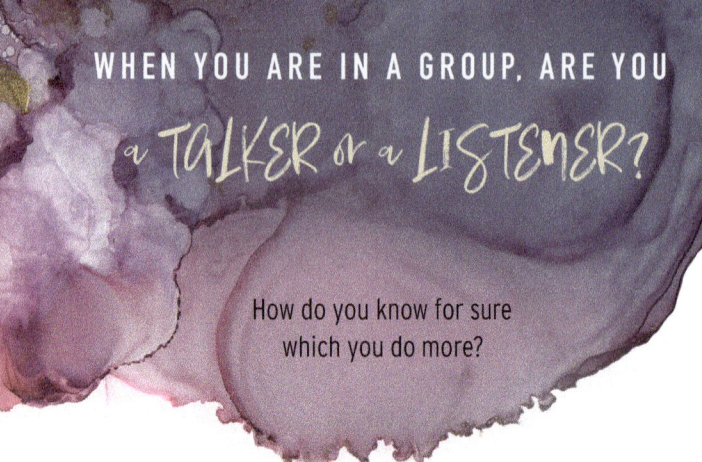

WHEN YOU ARE IN A GROUP, ARE YOU a TALKER or a LISTENER?

How do you know for sure which you do more?

Initial **thoughts & feelings** / One minute **rant**

I wonder and question...

What can we **carry forward** from the past?
What can we **leave behind**?

How do our **great-great-grandchildren** hope we answer this question?

I wonder what the **dominant culture** is telling me?

What is the part of this **I don't want to talk about?**
What are the stories I am telling myself?

What does your **heart** want?

  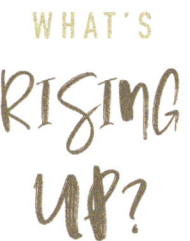  

This week, I intend to:

THE #1 CAUSE OF ELDER POVERTY IN THE UNITED STATES IS BEING A BIOLOGICAL MOTHER.

What changes can we make to ensure that all mothers and caregivers are taken care of?

I wonder and question...

Initial **thoughts & feelings** / One minute **rant**

What can we **carry forward** from the past?
What can we **leave behind**?

How do our **great-great-grandchildren** hope we answer this question?

I wonder what the **dominant culture** is telling me?

What is the part of this **I don't want to talk about?**
What are the stories I am telling myself?

What does your **heart** want?

  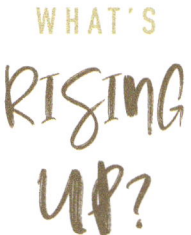  

This week, I intend to:

WHO HAS WRITTEN AND SPOKEN *the HISTORY you CARRY* WITH YOU?

Whose voices may have been left out, and how can we bring those voices into the cultural narrative?

I wonder and question...

Initial **thoughts & feelings** / One minute **rant**

What can we **carry forward** from the past?
What can we **leave behind**?

How do our **great-great-grandchildren**
hope we answer this question?

I wonder what the **dominant culture** is telling me?

What is the part of this **I don't want to talk about?**
What are the stories I am telling myself?

What does your **heart** want?

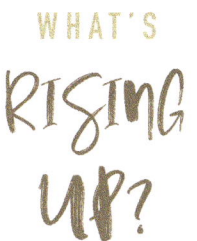

This week, I intend to:

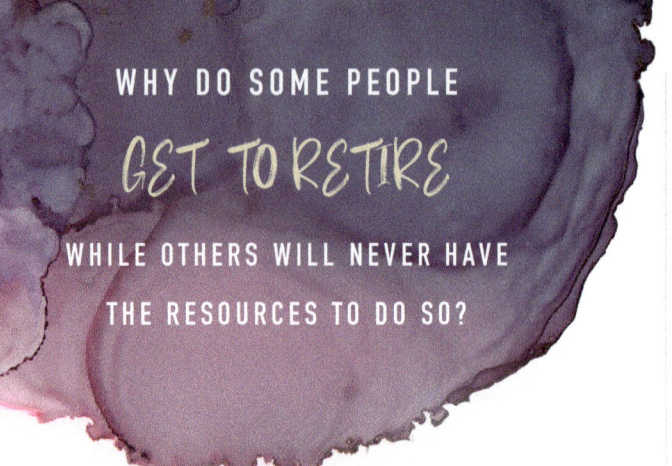

WHY DO SOME PEOPLE GET TO RETIRE WHILE OTHERS WILL NEVER HAVE THE RESOURCES TO DO SO?

Initial **thoughts & feelings** / One minute **rant**

I wonder and question...

What can we **carry forward** from the past?
What can we **leave behind**?

How do our **great-great-grandchildren**
hope we answer this question?

I wonder what the **dominant culture** is telling me?

What is the part of this **I don't want to talk about?**
What are the stories I am telling myself?

What does your **heart** want?

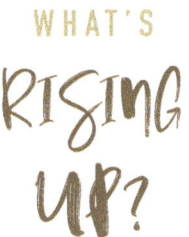

This week, I intend to:

WHAT WOULD IT BE LIKE
IF WE KNEW WELL-BEING
RESIDED AT THE INTERSECTION OF
INDEPENDENCE AND INTERDEPENDENCE.

THE PLACE WHERE
EACH OF OUR GIFTS
JOINS THE WORLD FOR
THE COLLECTIVE
GOOD OF ALL
LIVING THINGS.

WE, the PEOPLE

We, the People is remembering
we are all in this together.

Ultimately it's that simple.
On this planet, that is.

It's in our capacity to move from dominant systems
to ones that work for all living beings.

Stand for all.

We have power as a "we" that we don't have as an individual.
We don't use it often enough.

Our extreme individualism has rocked us to sleep.

We, the People and the Planet.

It's in our ancestry. If we go back to go forward.
And none too soon.

We can act collectively while cultivating ideas and thoughts
and feelings that come from individual creativity.

How do we harness our individual gifts in service
to creating a world that works for all?

We are a "we" whether we like it or not.

Our destiny is inexplicably linked.

WHAT DO YOU SEE AS THE MOST IMPORTANT ISSUE OF OUR TIME?

Initial **thoughts & feelings** / One minute **rant**

I wonder and question...

What can we **carry forward** from the past?
What can we **leave behind**?

How do our **great-great-grandchildren**
hope we answer this question?

I wonder what the **dominant culture** is telling me?

What is the part of this **I don't want to talk about?**
What are the stories I am telling myself?

What does your **heart** want?

  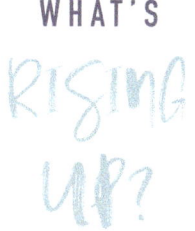  

WHAT'S RISING UP?

HOW TO BE?   WHAT TO DO?   WHAT TO HAVE/KNOW?   WHAT TO IMAGINE…

This week, I intend to:

WHAT ARE YOUR CONCERNS FOR THE *MOST VULNERABLE* POPULATIONS?

How do we bring them to the table?
How do we give voice to those
who don't have a human voice?

I wonder and question...

Initial **thoughts & feelings** / One minute **rant**

What can we **carry forward** from the past?
What can we **leave behind**?

How do our **great-great-grandchildren**
hope we answer this question?

I wonder what the **dominant culture** is telling me?

What is the part of this **I don't want to talk about?**
What are the stories I am telling myself?

What does your **heart** want?

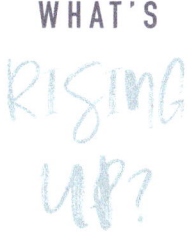

WHAT'S RISING UP?

HOW TO BE? WHAT TO DO? WHAT TO HAVE/KNOW? WHAT TO IMAGINE...

This week, I intend to:

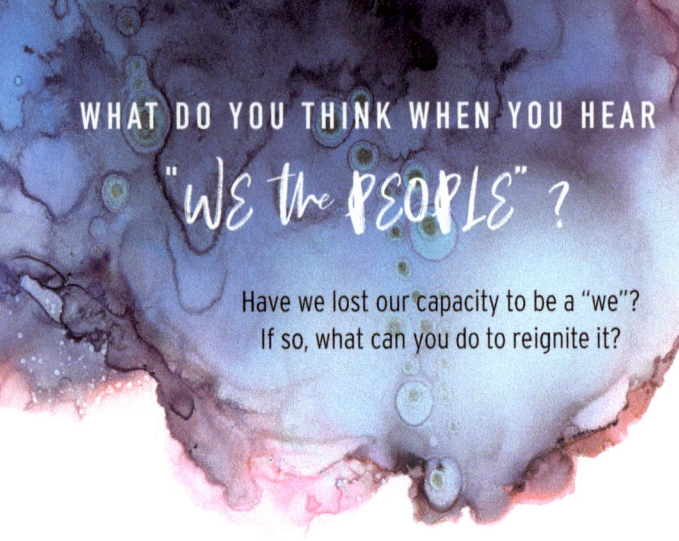

WHAT DO YOU THINK WHEN YOU HEAR "WE the PEOPLE"?

Have we lost our capacity to be a "we"?
If so, what can you do to reignite it?

Initial **thoughts & feelings** / One minute **rant**

I wonder and question...

What can we **carry forward** from the past?
What can we **leave behind?**

How do our **great-great-grandchildren**
hope we answer this question?

I wonder what the **dominant culture** is telling me?

What is the part of this **I don't want to talk about?**
What are the stories I am telling myself?

What does your **heart** want?

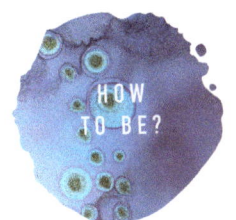  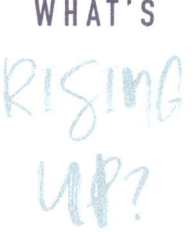  

WHAT'S RISING UP?

HOW TO BE? — WHAT TO DO? — WHAT TO HAVE/KNOW? — WHAT TO IMAGINE...

This week, I intend to:

HOW CAN YOU MAKE THE WORLD SAFER for WOMEN & GIRLS?

Initial **thoughts & feelings** / One minute **rant**

I wonder and question...

What can we **carry forward** from the past?
What can we **leave behind?**

How do our **great-great-grandchildren**
hope we answer this question?

I wonder what the **dominant culture** is telling me?

What is the part of this **I don't want to talk about?**
What are the stories I am telling myself?

What does your **heart** want?

  WHAT'S RISING UP?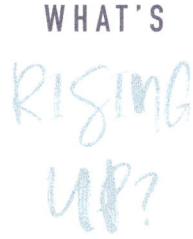

HOW TO BE? WHAT TO DO?   WHAT TO HAVE/KNOW? WHAT TO IMAGINE...

This week, I intend to:

DO SHAME AND GUILT ABOUT
NOT HAVING DONE ENOUGH
PREVENT YOU FROM TAKING ACTION NOW?

If so, what can you do to change that?

I wonder and question...

Initial **thoughts & feelings** / One minute **rant**

What can we **carry forward** from the past?
What can we **leave behind**?

How do our **great-great-grandchildren**
hope we answer this question?

I wonder what the **dominant culture** is telling me?

What is the part of this **I don't want to talk about?**
What are the stories I am telling myself?

What does your **heart** want?

  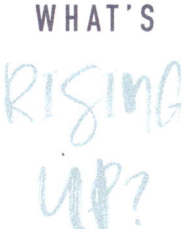  

WHAT'S RISING UP?

This week, I intend to:

WHAT IF THE CLOUDS SPELLED **REVERENCE**
AND IT WAS WRITTEN IN THE DIRT,
AND THE WAVES IN THE RIVER SHOUTED IT,
AND THE BIRDS IN THE TREES SANG IT,
AND THE SNOW COVERED TREES WERE ENVELOPED IN IT,

AND IT WAS TATTOOED ON OUR HEARTS.

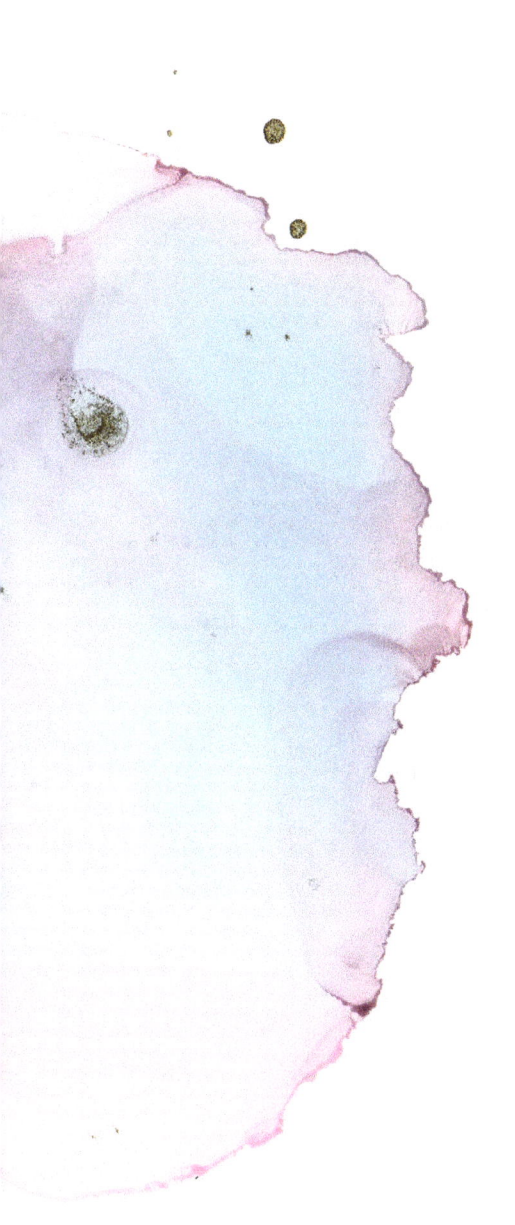

The MORE than HUMAN WORLD

Any living being that isn't human.

And the energy field around us. Spirit.
Much of what we don't know.

We live in anthropocentric times.

Our extreme individualism,
our self-centeredness, has an impact.

Our loss of reverence for all living beings.

There is mystery and magic in the more than human world.

The more than human world needs our deepest,
most imaginative listening.

To let go of knowing and lean into wonder, awe, reverence
and the sacred.

Our interconnectedness.

IF THE PRICE OF OUR CONSUMER PRODUCTS INCLUDED AND IDENTIFIED THE COST to the ENVIRONMENT, WOULD YOUR PURCHASING HABITS CHANGE?

How could we fairly distribute that cost?

I wonder and question...

Initial **thoughts & feelings** / One minute **rant**

What can we **carry forward** from the past?
What can we **leave behind**?

How do our **great-great-grandchildren** hope we answer this question?

I wonder what the **dominant culture** is telling me?

What is the part of this **I don't want to talk about?**
What are the stories I am telling myself?

What does your **heart** want?

  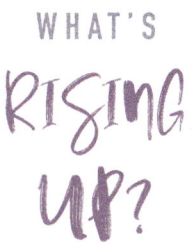  

This week, I intend to:

HOW IS YOUR PERSONAL HEALTH CONNECTED TO THE NATURAL WORLD?

Initial **thoughts & feelings** / One minute **rant**

I wonder and question...

What can we **carry forward** from the past?
What can we **leave behind?**

How do our **great-great-grandchildren**
hope we answer this question?

I wonder what the **dominant culture** is telling me?

What is the part of this **I don't want to talk about?**
What are the stories I am telling myself?

What does your **heart** want?

  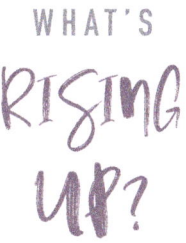  

This week, I intend to:

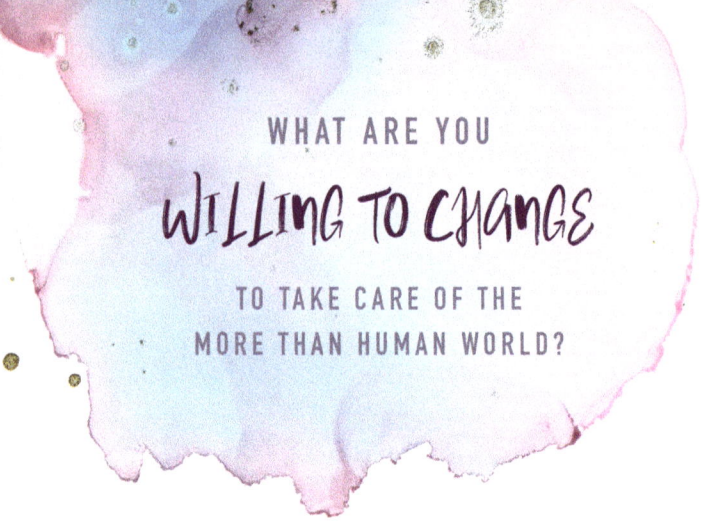

WHAT ARE YOU **WILLING TO CHANGE** TO TAKE CARE OF THE MORE THAN HUMAN WORLD?

I wonder and question...

Initial **thoughts & feelings** / One minute **rant**

What can we **carry forward** from the past?
What can we **leave behind**?

How do our **great-great-grandchildren**
hope we answer this question?

I wonder what the **dominant culture** is telling me?

What is the part of this **I don't want to talk about?**
What are the stories I am telling myself?

What does your **heart** want?

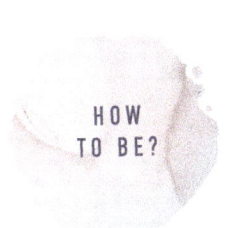

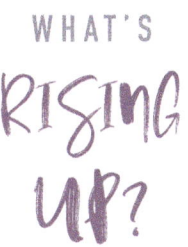

This week, I intend to:

HOW COULD YOU REDEFINE FUN SO IT INCLUDED TAKING CARE OF YOURSELF AND THE WORLD AROUND YOU?

I wonder and question...

Initial **thoughts & feelings** / One minute **rant**

What can we **carry forward** from the past?
What can we **leave behind?**

How do our **great-great-grandchildren**
hope we answer this question?

I wonder what the **dominant culture** is telling me?

What is the part of this **I don't want to talk about**?
What are the stories I am telling myself?

What does your **heart** want?

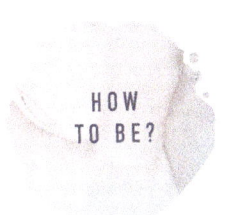

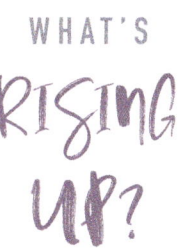

This week, I intend to:

WHAT COULD YOU DO TO HELP OTHERS HAVE REVERENCE for NATURE INSTEAD OF SEEING IT PRIMARILY AS A RESOURCE AND RECREATIONAL LANDSCAPE FOR HUMANS?

Initial **thoughts & feelings** / One minute **rant**

I wonder and question…

What can we **carry forward** from the past?
What can we **leave behind?**

How do our **great-great-grandchildren** hope we answer this question?

I wonder what the **dominant culture** is telling me?

What is the part of this **I don't want to talk about?**
What are the stories I am telling myself?

What does your **heart** want?

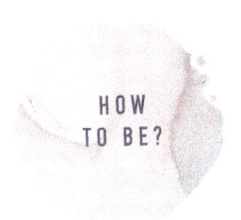

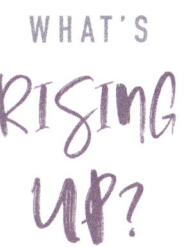

HOW TO BE? — WHAT TO DO? — WHAT'S RISING UP? — WHAT TO HAVE/KNOW? — WHAT TO IMAGINE...

This week, I intend to:

WHAT'S YOUR RELATIONSHIP WITH
FOSSIL FUELS?

Initial **thoughts & feelings** / One minute **rant**

I wonder and question...

What can we **carry forward** from the past?
What can we **leave behind?**

How do our **great-great-grandchildren**
hope we answer this question?

I wonder what the **dominant culture** is telling me?

What is the part of this **I don't want to talk about?**
What are the stories I am telling myself?

What does your **heart** want?

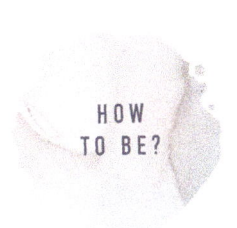  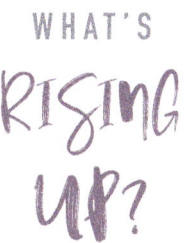  

This week, I intend to:

WHAT RIGHTS WOULD YOU LIKE TO SEE **PROTECTED or RECOGNIZED** FOR THE MORE THAN HUMAN WORLD?

Initial **thoughts & feelings** / One minute **rant**

I wonder and question...

What can we **carry forward** from the past?
What can we **leave behind**?

How do our **great-great-grandchildren**
hope we answer this question?

I wonder what the **dominant culture** is telling me?

What is the part of this **I don't want to talk about?**
What are the stories I am telling myself?

What does your **heart** want?

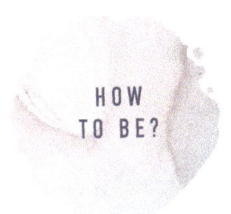  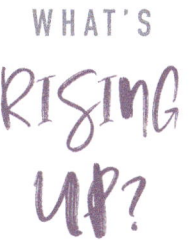  

This week, I intend to:

OUR CULTURE TENDS TO FOCUS ON MONEY ABOVE ALL ELSE.

IT HAS BECOME HOW WE MEASURE OUR LIFE: MUCH MORE SO THAN WHAT WE HAVE SHARED, GIVEN, OR OFFERED THE WORLD.

Legacy

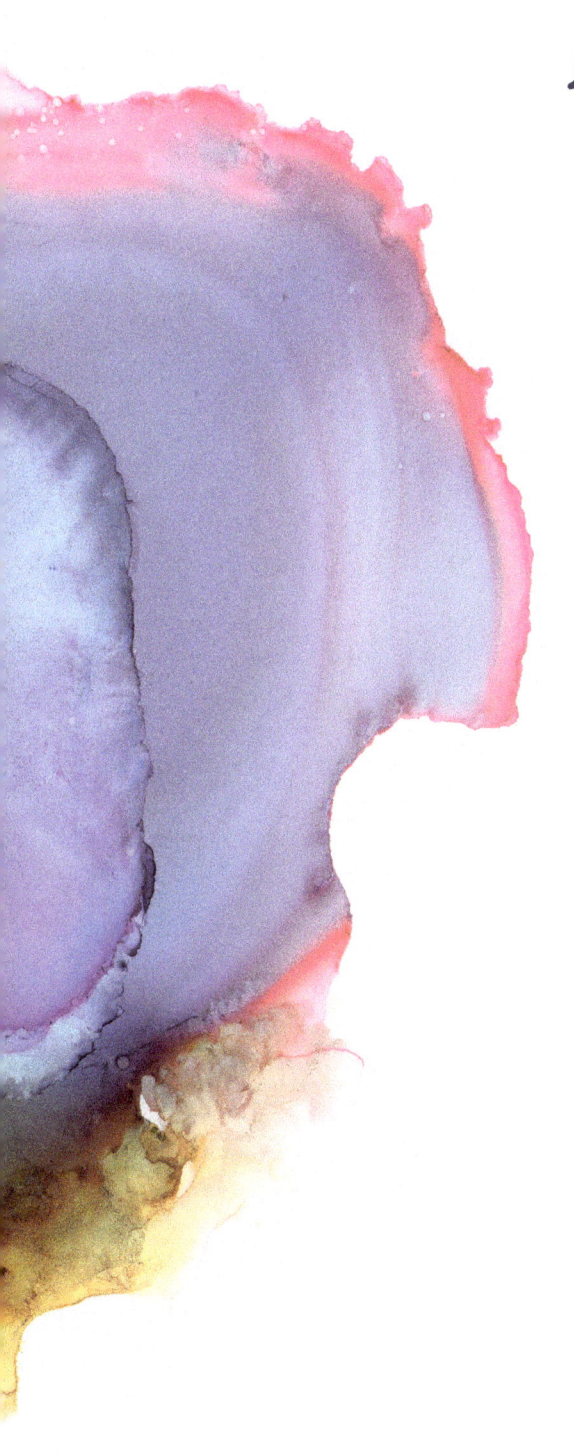

We are the ancestors of the future.

The future of humanity and the future of the more than human world.

Legacy is deep and wide, a lifetime, and every lived moment.

It is the day-to-day choices.

It is the thoughts we tell ourselves.

And what we share with others.

It's scarily relevant and on some level, perhaps, forgiving.

Getting up everyday and remembering this could be my last day, my last breath.

Coming back to presence again and again.

Falling down 100 times and getting up 101.

A living legacy is a practice.

Inhabiting… *"It's more than this lifetime."*

It's beyond me and you.

It's the grains of sand in the hourglass of our days.

It's the footprints I won't see.

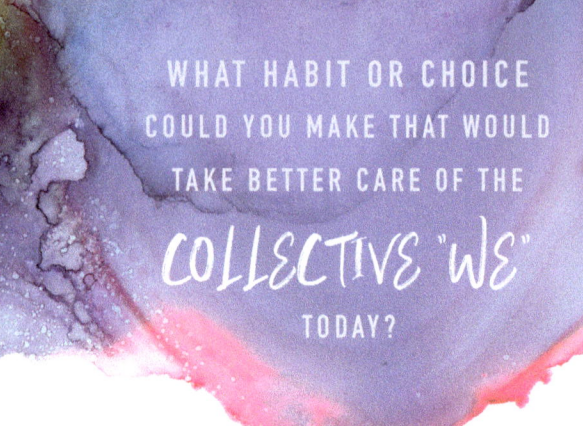

WHAT HABIT OR CHOICE COULD YOU MAKE THAT WOULD TAKE BETTER CARE OF THE *COLLECTIVE "WE"* TODAY?

Initial **thoughts & feelings** / One minute **rant**

I wonder and question...

What can we **carry forward** from the past?
What can we **leave behind**?

How do our **great-great-grandchildren**
hope we answer this question?

I wonder what the **dominant culture** is telling me?

What is the part of this **I don't want to talk about?**
What are the stories I am telling myself?

What does your **heart** want?

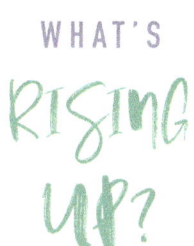

WHAT'S RISING UP?

HOW TO BE?
WHAT TO DO?
WHAT TO HAVE/KNOW?
WHAT TO IMAGINE…

This week, I intend to:

HOW WILL YOUR LEGACY **SUPPORT** *the* **FUTURE** OF OUR CHILDRENS' CHILDREN?

Initial **thoughts & feelings** / One minute **rant**

I wonder and question...

What can we **carry forward** from the past?
What can we **leave behind**?

How do our **great-great-grandchildren**
hope we answer this question?

I wonder what the **dominant culture** is telling me?

What is the part of this **I don't want to talk about?**
What are the stories I am telling myself?

What does your **heart** want?

  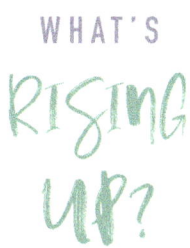  

This week, I intend to:

WHAT DO YOU SEE AS YOUR GREATEST CONTRIBUTION SO FAR?

I wonder and question...

Initial **thoughts & feelings** / One minute **rant**

What can we **carry forward** from the past?
What can we **leave behind?**

How do our **great-great-grandchildren**
hope we answer this question?

I wonder what the **dominant culture** is telling me?

What is the part of this **I don't want to talk about?**
What are the stories I am telling myself?

What does your **heart** want?

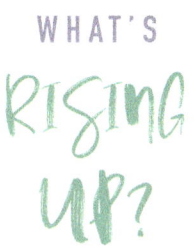

This week, I intend to:

HOW AND WHERE ARE YOU INVESTING YOUR MONEY?

How do my investments impact the environment?

How do my investments support women and children?

I wonder and question...

Initial **thoughts & feelings** / One minute **rant**

What can we **carry forward** from the past?
What can we **leave behind**?

How do our **great-great-grandchildren** hope we answer this question?

I wonder what the **dominant culture** is telling me?

What is the part of this **I don't want to talk about?**
What are the stories I am telling myself?

What does your **heart** want?

  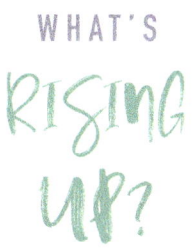  

HOW TO BE? · WHAT TO DO? · WHAT'S RISING UP? · WHAT TO HAVE/KNOW? · WHAT TO IMAGINE...

This week, I intend to:

WHAT ARE THE QUALITIES YOU WANT TO BE REMEMBERED FOR?

How do those qualities support a world that works for all?

I wonder and question...

Initial **thoughts & feelings** / One minute **rant**

What can we **carry forward** from the past?
What can we **leave behind**?

How do our **great-great-grandchildren**
hope we answer this question?

I wonder what the **dominant culture** is telling me?

What is the part of this **I don't want to talk about?**
What are the stories I am telling myself?

What does your **heart** want?

  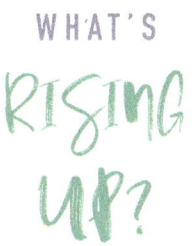  

This week, I intend to:

WE COMMUNED IN THE WAYS INFANTS CAN,
THROUGH TOUCH, SMILES, COOS AND LAUGHTER, CRIES AND HUGS.

WE GAZED DEEPLY INTO EACH OTHER'S EYES
FOR LONG INTERRUPTED MOMENTS.

WHICH WAS LIKE
DROPPING INTO
A BEAUTIFUL,
UNENDING POOL
OF LOVE.

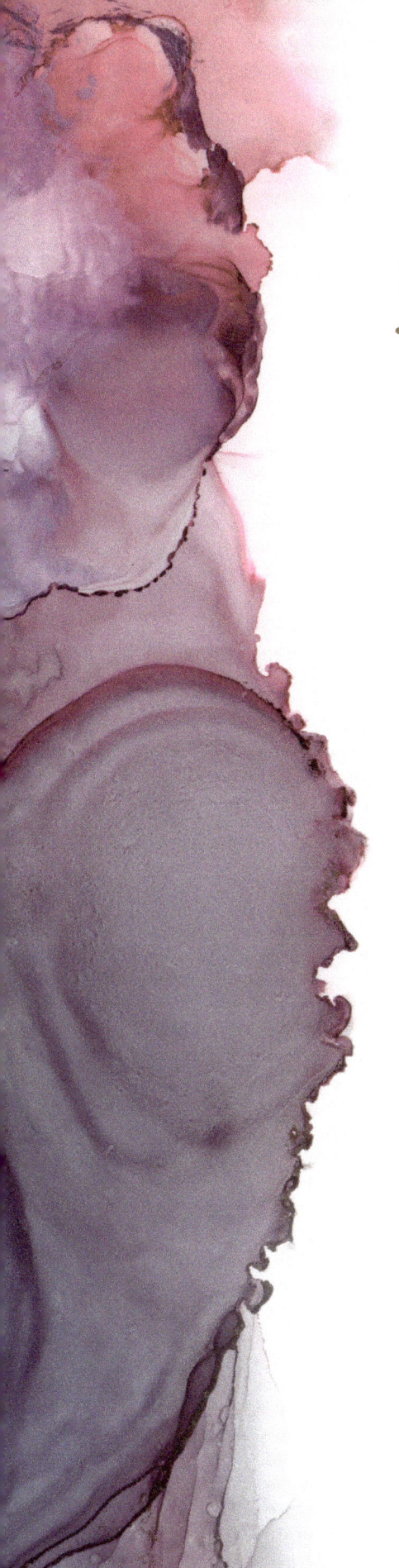

BELONGING

When we truly, deeply, madly belong to ourselves there are no boundaries to belonging.

No walls even if they are there.
That's a steep path.
And our work is to belong everywhere.
We don't have to like someone or something for them to belong.
Spiders belong and I try and live harmoniously with them.

We are natural. We are nature.
We belong to her first.
We've forsaken that.
The living breathing earth first. We are earth. We are breath.
And we are each other's keepers.

Be your longing.
Belonging is reverence embodied.
Dare I say there is a sacredness to belonging?
When we exclude any part of ourselves we exclude that in all we see.
Belonging to our flaws and our gifts.
Belonging is a deep need to be seen, heard and acknowledged.

We exist.
We belong.

WHO ARE THE PEOPLE IN YOUR LIFE THAT *FILL YOU UP?*

How much face-to-face time do you have with them each week?

Initial **thoughts & feelings** / One minute **rant**

I wonder and question...

What can we **carry forward** from the past?
What can we **leave behind?**

How do our **great-great-grandchildren**
hope we answer this question?

I wonder what the **dominant culture** is telling me?

What is the part of this **I don't want to talk about?**
What are the stories I am telling myself?

What does your **heart** want?

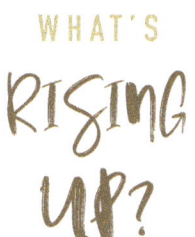

This week, I intend to:

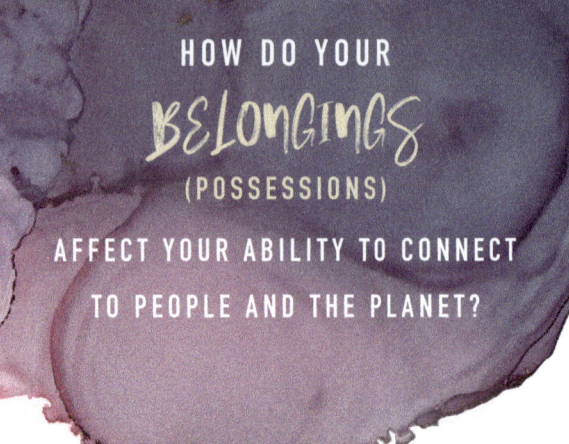

HOW DO YOUR BELONGINGS (POSSESSIONS) AFFECT YOUR ABILITY TO CONNECT TO PEOPLE AND THE PLANET?

Initial **thoughts & feelings** / One minute **rant**

I wonder and question...

What can we **carry forward** from the past?
What can we **leave behind**?

How do our **great-great-grandchildren**
hope we answer this question?

I wonder what the **dominant culture** is telling me?

What is the part of this **I don't want to talk about?**
What are the stories I am telling myself?

What does your **heart** want?

  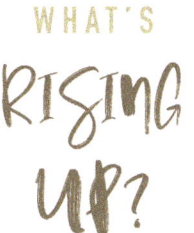  

This week, I intend to:

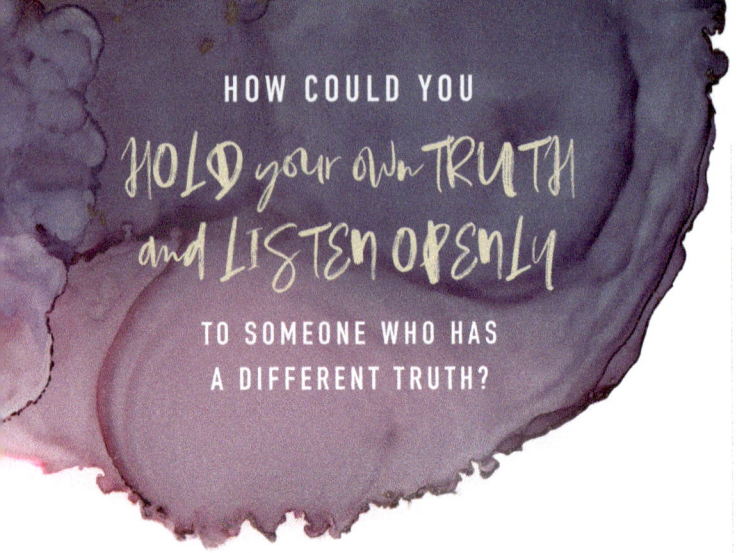

HOW COULD YOU **HOLD** your own **TRUTH** and **LISTEN OPENLY** TO SOMEONE WHO HAS A DIFFERENT TRUTH?

Initial **thoughts & feelings** / One minute **rant**

I wonder and question...

What can we **carry forward** from the past?
What can we **leave behind?**

How do our **great-great-grandchildren**
hope we answer this question?

I wonder what the **dominant culture** is telling me?

What is the part of this **I don't want to talk about?**
What are the stories I am telling myself?

What does your **heart** want?

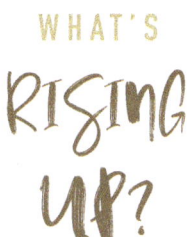

This week, I intend to:

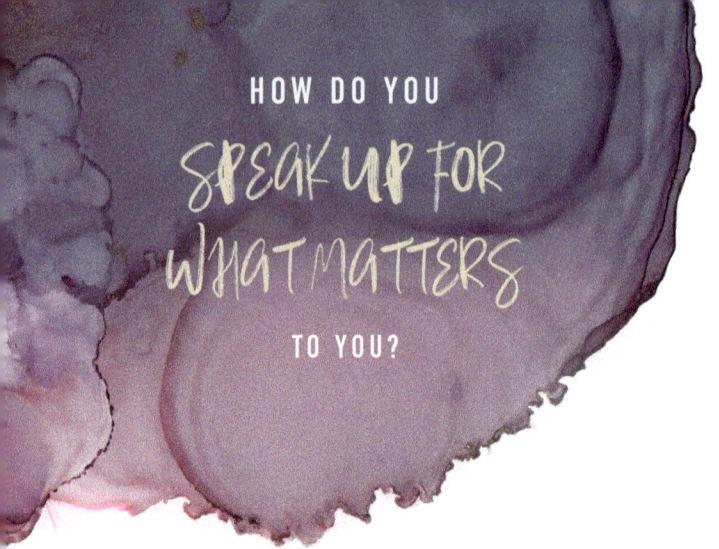

HOW DO YOU SPEAK UP FOR WHAT MATTERS TO YOU?

I wonder and question...

Initial **thoughts & feelings** / One minute **rant**

What can we **carry forward** from the past?
What can we **leave behind**?

How do our **great-great-grandchildren**
hope we answer this question?

I wonder what the **dominant culture** is telling me?

What is the part of this **I don't want to talk about?**
What are the stories I am telling myself?

What does your **heart** want?

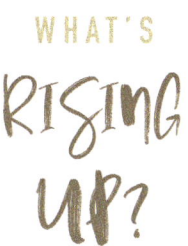

This week, I intend to:

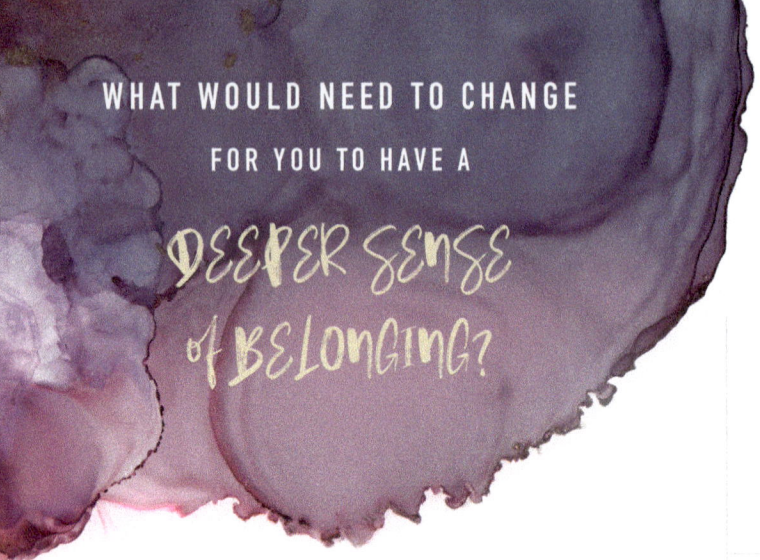

WHAT WOULD NEED TO CHANGE FOR YOU TO HAVE A *DEEPER SENSE of BELONGING?*

I wonder and question...

Initial **thoughts & feelings** / One minute **rant**

What can we **carry forward** from the past?
What can we **leave behind?**

How do our **great-great-grandchildren**
hope we answer this question?

I wonder what the **dominant culture** is telling me?

What is the part of this **I don't want to talk about?**
What are the stories I am telling myself?

What does your **heart** want?

  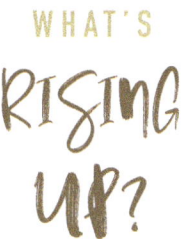  

This week, I intend to:

WE BELIEVE LOVING AND LIVING THE QUESTIONS IS A DOORWAY TO POSSIBILITIES BEYOND OUR WILDEST IMAGINATION.

LET'S CULTIVATE A CONSCIOUSNESS OF INTERCONNECTIVITY. OF ME AND WE. OF A TIMELESS FRESH TOGETHERNESS OLDER THAN TIME.

COMMUNITY

A grove of trees. A gaggle of geese.

A group of people who are committed to
caring and sharing time, energy, and resources.

It's not about "alikeness" or sameness.
Diversity accepted and embraced.

A willingness to work…together.

Committed to me and we.
Self and others.
Inter-being.

A world where we can be alone together
and have deeply alive relationships.

Inclusive of the
more than human world.

WHAT IS THE MOST PRESSING ISSUE IN YOUR COMMUNITY?

Initial **thoughts & feelings** / One minute **rant**

I wonder and question...

What can we **carry forward** from the past?
What can we **leave behind?**

How do our **great-great-grandchildren**
hope we answer this question?

I wonder what the **dominant culture** is telling me?

What is the part of this **I don't want to talk about?**
What are the stories I am telling myself?

What does your **heart** want?

  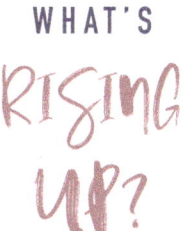  

This week, I intend to:

HOW DO YOU EXTEND YOUR CARE BEYOND YOUR PRIVATE LIFE?

How do you extend care towards who and what you don't know or isn't familiar?

How do you care for nature and the more than human world?

I wonder and question...

Initial **thoughts & feelings** / One minute **rant**

What can we **carry forward** from the past?
What can we **leave behind**?

How do our **great-great-grandchildren** hope we answer this question?

I wonder what the **dominant culture** is telling me?

What is the part of this **I don't want to talk about?**
What are the stories I am telling myself?

What does your **heart** want?

  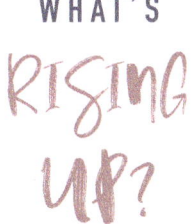  

HOW TO BE? — WHAT TO DO? — WHAT'S RISING UP? — WHAT TO HAVE/KNOW? — WHAT TO IMAGINE…

This week, I intend to:

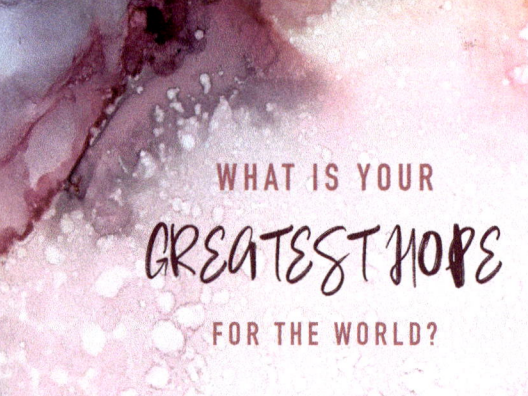

WHAT IS YOUR GREATEST HOPE FOR THE WORLD?

I wonder and question...

Initial **thoughts & feelings** / One minute **rant**

What can we **carry forward** from the past?
What can we **leave behind?**

How do our **great-great-grandchildren**
hope we answer this question?

I wonder what the **dominant culture** is telling me?

What is the part of this **I don't want to talk about?**
What are the stories I am telling myself?

What does your **heart** want?

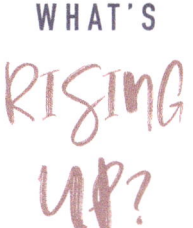

This week, I intend to:

HOW DO YOU MEASURE GIVING BACK TO YOUR COMMUNITY?

Initial **thoughts & feelings** / One minute **rant**

I wonder and question...

What can we **carry forward** from the past?
What can we **leave behind**?

How do our **great-great-grandchildren**
hope we answer this question?

I wonder what the **dominant culture** is telling me?

What is the part of this **I don't want to talk about?**
What are the stories I am telling myself?

What does your **heart** want?

  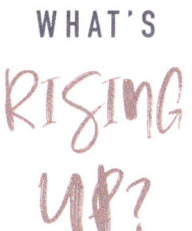  

This week, I intend to:

NAME SOMEONE IN YOUR COMMUNITY WHO INSPIRES YOU.

What are their qualities and how could you cultivate those in your own life?

Initial **thoughts & feelings** / One minute **rant**

I wonder and question...

What can we **carry forward** from the past?
What can we **leave behind**?

How do our **great-great-grandchildren**
hope we answer this question?

I wonder what the **dominant culture** is telling me?

What is the part of this **I don't want to talk about?**
What are the stories I am telling myself?

What does your **heart** want?

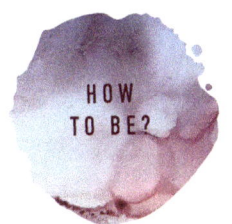  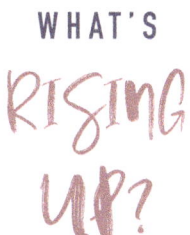  

HOW TO BE? — WHAT TO DO? — WHAT'S RISING UP? — WHAT TO HAVE/KNOW? — WHAT TO IMAGINE...

This week, I intend to:

EVERYONE WANTS TO BE
SEEN, HEARD, AND ACKNOWLEDGED
FOR WHO THEY ARE.

THAT IS THE WORLD WE ARE FOSTERING.

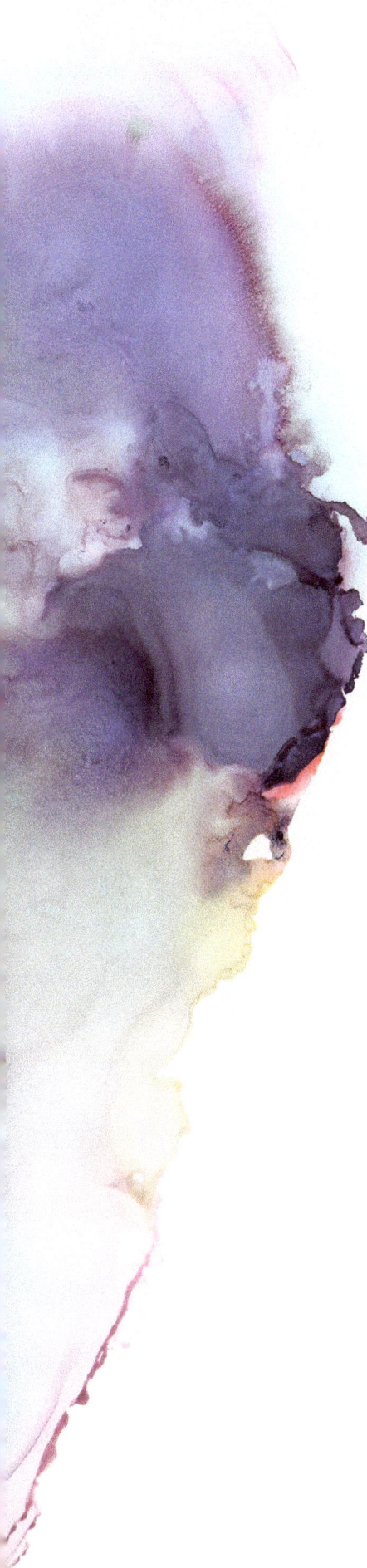

Inclusivity

Welcoming all.
And everything.

It's not about inviting everyone to everything or everywhere.

It's not about agreeing with everyone.

It's not about liking.

It's about honoring that there is room in the world for all.

It's the fabric we weave together that allows for our differences to sit beside our sameness.

All living beings.

An awareness of how we create separation.

A willingness to examine the flawed systems we live in and under.

An intention to include what's been excluded.

SHARE AN EXPERIENCE OF GETTING TO KNOW SOMEONE **you saw as "OTHER"** AND HAVING A CHANGE OF HEART ABOUT THEM.

How did you bridge the gap between your differences?

Initial **thoughts & feelings** / One minute **rant**

I wonder and question...

What can we **carry forward** from the past?
What can we **leave behind**?

How do our **great-great-grandchildren**
hope we answer this question?

I wonder what the **dominant culture** is telling me?

What is the part of this **I don't want to talk about?**
What are the stories I am telling myself?

What does your **heart** want?

WHAT'S RISING UP?

This week, I intend to:

HOW DO YOU CULTIVATE OR NURTURE RELATIONSHIPS WITH THE MORE THAN HUMAN WORLD?

I wonder and question...

Initial thoughts & feelings / One minute **rant**

What can we **carry forward** from the past?
What can we **leave behind**?

How do our **great-great-grandchildren** hope we answer this question?

I wonder what the **dominant culture** is telling me?

What is the part of this **I don't want to talk about?**
What are the stories I am telling myself?

What does your **heart** want?

 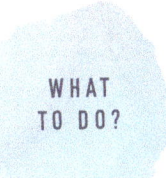 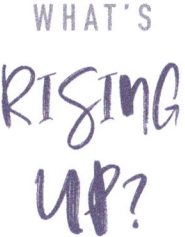  

HOW TO BE? — WHAT TO DO? — WHAT'S RISING UP? — WHAT TO HAVE/KNOW? — WHAT TO IMAGINE...

This week, I intend to:

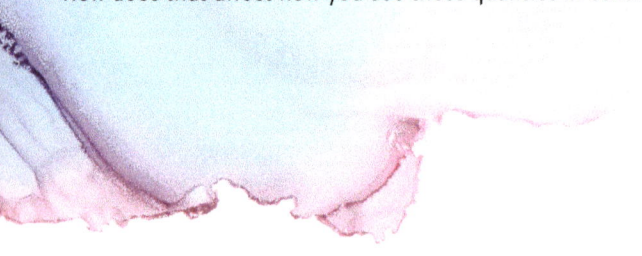

WHAT PARTS OF YOURSELF DO YOU EXCLUDE or HIDE AWAY?

How does that affect how you see those qualities in others?

Initial **thoughts & feelings** / One minute **rant**

I wonder and question...

What can we **carry forward** from the past?
What can we **leave behind**?

How do our **great-great-grandchildren**
hope we answer this question?

I wonder what the **dominant culture** is telling me?

What is the part of this **I don't want to talk about?**
What are the stories I am telling myself?

What does your **heart** want?

 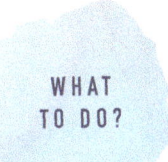 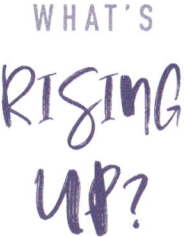  

WHAT'S RISING UP?

HOW TO BE?

WHAT TO DO?

WHAT TO HAVE/KNOW?

WHAT TO IMAGINE...

This week, I intend to:

WRITE ABOUT A TIME WHEN

YOU WERE INCLUDED.

What did you take away from that experience?

Initial **thoughts & feelings** / One minute **rant**

I wonder and question...

What can we **carry forward** from the past?
What can we **leave behind?**

How do our **great-great-grandchildren**
hope we answer this question?

I wonder what the **dominant culture** is telling me?

What is the part of this **I don't want to talk about?**
What are the stories I am telling myself?

What does your **heart** want?

  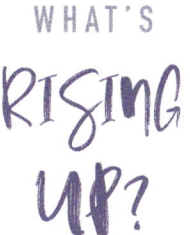  

HOW TO BE? WHAT TO DO? WHAT'S RISING UP? WHAT TO HAVE/KNOW? WHAT TO IMAGINE...

This week, I intend to:

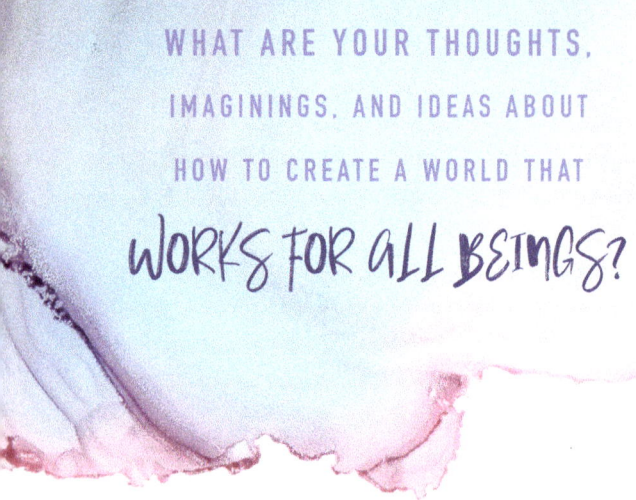

WHAT ARE YOUR THOUGHTS, IMAGININGS, AND IDEAS ABOUT HOW TO CREATE A WORLD THAT *Works for all beings?*

Initial **thoughts & feelings** / One minute **rant**

I wonder and question...

What can we **carry forward** from the past?
What can we **leave behind**?

How do our **great-great-grandchildren** hope we answer this question?

I wonder what the **dominant culture** is telling me?

What is the part of this **I don't want to talk about?**
What are the stories I am telling myself?

What does your **heart** want?

 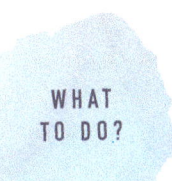 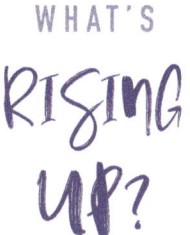  

HOW TO BE? — WHAT TO DO? — WHAT'S RISING UP? — WHAT TO HAVE/KNOW? — WHAT TO IMAGINE...

This week, I intend to:

WE SHARED THE BIKE
BECAUSE IT WAS WHAT WE HAD.
ONE BIKE FOR THREE OF US.

WE DIDN'T COMPLAIN
ABOUT NOT HAVING
ANOTHER ONE.

WE DIDN'T GO OFF ON OUR OWN.

WE FOUND A WAY TO
BE TOGETHER,
WORK TOGETHER,
SHARE OUR RESOURCE,
AND HAVE A BLAST DOING IT.

CONNECTIVITY

The innate and infinite knowing that everything is inexplicably linked to everything else.

The moments I live from that place in my body
Are the moments I am closest to being whole.

Connectivity is not saying there is no individuality.
It is saying that in the individual lives the collective.
And in the collective the individual.

Not either/or.
It's both/and.
It's delicious.

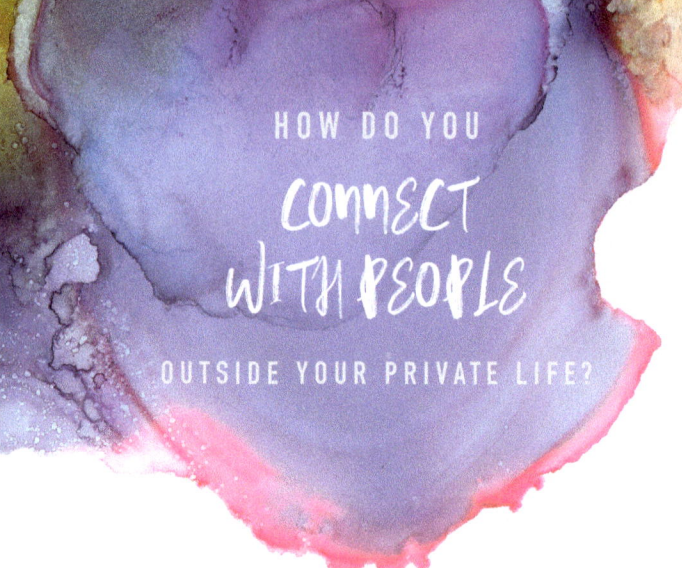

HOW DO YOU CONNECT WITH PEOPLE OUTSIDE YOUR PRIVATE LIFE?

I wonder and question…

Initial **thoughts & feelings** / One minute **rant**

What can we **carry forward** from the past?
What can we **leave behind?**

How do our **great-great-grandchildren**
hope we answer this question?

I wonder what the **dominant culture** is telling me?

What is the part of this **I don't want to talk about?**
What are the stories I am telling myself?

What does your **heart** want?

  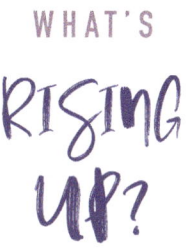  

This week, I intend to:

WHEN ARE YOU VULNERABLE?

When have you seen someone's vulnerability as courage?

How could being vulnerable support you and the world?

I wonder and question...

Initial **thoughts & feelings** / One minute **rant**

What can we **carry forward** from the past?
What can we **leave behind**?

How do our **great-great-grandchildren** hope we answer this question?

I wonder what the **dominant culture** is telling me?

What is the part of this **I don't want to talk about?**
What are the stories I am telling myself?

What does your **heart** want?

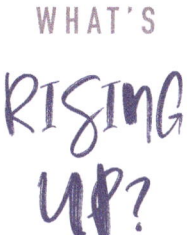

WHAT'S RISING UP?

HOW TO BE?

WHAT TO DO?

WHAT TO HAVE/KNOW?

WHAT TO IMAGINE...

This week, I intend to:

HOW DO YOU HOLD BOTH INDEPENDENCE & INTERDEPENDENCE?

What needs to change in the United States for us to have a healthier balance between the two?

I wonder and question...

Initial **thoughts & feelings** / One minute **rant**

What can we **carry forward** from the past?
What can we **leave behind**?

How do our **great-great-grandchildren** hope we answer this question?

I wonder what the **dominant culture** is telling me?

What is the part of this **I don't want to talk about?**
What are the stories I am telling myself?

What does your **heart** want?

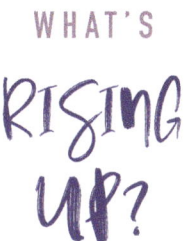

WHAT'S RISING UP?

HOW TO BE? WHAT TO DO? WHAT TO HAVE/KNOW? WHAT TO IMAGINE...

This week, I intend to:

WHAT DO YOU DO TO TAKE CARE OF YOUR PERSONAL HEALTH?

Can you add a practice that includes taking care of the more than human world?

I wonder and question...

Initial **thoughts & feelings** / One minute **rant**

What can we **carry forward** from the past?
What can we **leave behind**?

How do our **great-great-grandchildren**
hope we answer this question?

I wonder what the **dominant culture** is telling me?

What is the part of this **I don't want to talk about?**
What are the stories I am telling myself?

What does your **heart** want?

  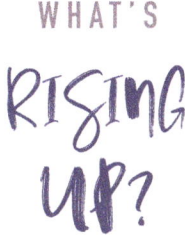  

This week, I intend to:

HOW DO YOU HOLD BOTH *ME & Mine* AND *WE & Ours* WHEN A PERSONAL DECISION AFFECTS THE WELL-BEING OF OTHERS?

I wonder and question…

Initial **thoughts & feelings** / One minute **rant**

What can we **carry forward** from the past?
What can we **leave behind**?

How do our **great-great-grandchildren** hope we answer this question?

I wonder what the **dominant culture** is telling me?

What is the part of this **I don't want to talk about?**
What are the stories I am telling myself?

What does your **heart** want?

  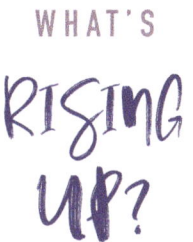  

WHAT'S RISING UP?

This week, I intend to:

SO WHATEVER IT IS YOU DO THAT HELPS WIDEN YOUR LENS,
DO THAT.

GET BEYOND YOUR OWN PERSPECTIVE.
SEE THROUGH THE LENS OF
A TREE,
A CHILD,

SOMEONE YOU DISAGREE WITH.

Compassion

Being with yourself or another living being with the intention of being fully present.

To bear witness.
Sometimes fierce and fiery.
Sometimes tender and soft.
Or anywhere in between.
Action.
Presence truly and deeply, is action.
To do or be in a way that supports the alleviation of suffering.
A quality of aliveness.

A cultivation of the deepest strands of our heart.

SHARE A TIME WHEN YOU GAVE
OR RECEIVED WITH AN

OPEN HEART.

What did you take away from that experience?

Initial **thoughts & feelings** / One minute **rant**

I wonder and question...

What can we **carry forward** from the past?
What can we **leave behind?**

How do our **great-great-grandchildren**
hope we answer this question?

I wonder what the **dominant culture** is telling me?

What is the part of this **I don't want to talk about?**
What are the stories I am telling myself?

What does your **heart** want?

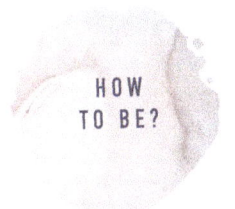    

HOW TO BE?   WHAT TO DO?   WHAT'S RISING UP?   WHAT TO HAVE/KNOW?   WHAT TO IMAGINE...

This week, I intend to:

HAS YOUR HEART BEEN BROKEN?

Did it break open or apart?

Has it changed how you see others when their hearts are broken? *If yes, say more about that.*

I wonder and question...

Initial **thoughts & feelings** / One minute **rant**

What can we **carry forward** from the past?
What can we **leave behind?**

How do our **great-great-grandchildren**
hope we answer this question?

I wonder what the **dominant culture** is telling me?

What is the part of this **I don't want to talk about**?
What are the stories I am telling myself?

What does your **heart** want?

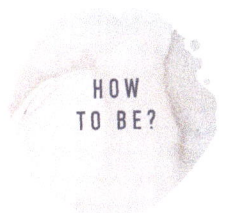   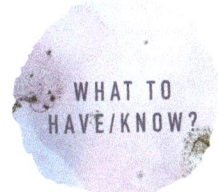 

HOW TO BE? — WHAT TO DO? — WHAT'S RISING UP? — WHAT TO HAVE/KNOW? — WHAT TO IMAGINE...

This week, I intend to:

HOW DO YOU RESPOND TO THE *SUFFERING OF ANOTHER* LIVING BEING?

I wonder and question...

Initial **thoughts & feelings** / One minute **rant**

What can we **carry forward** from the past?
What can we **leave behind?**

How do our **great-great-grandchildren**
hope we answer this question?

I wonder what the **dominant culture** is telling me?

What is the part of this **I don't want to talk about**?
What are the stories I am telling myself?

What does your **heart** want?

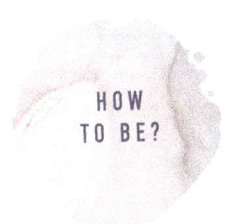

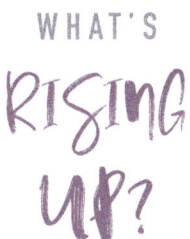

This week, I intend to:

WHEN YOU SAY ONE THING AND

DO ANOTHER,

HOW DOES YOUR HEART FEEL?

How do you take care of your heart?

Initial **thoughts & feelings** / One minute **rant**

I wonder and question...

What can we **carry forward** from the past?
What can we **leave behind**?

How do our **great-great-grandchildren**
hope we answer this question?

I wonder what the **dominant culture** is telling me?

What is the part of this **I don't want to talk about?**
What are the stories I am telling myself?

What does your **heart** want?

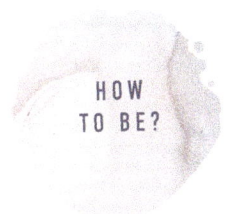

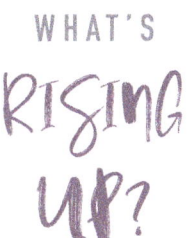

This week, I intend to:

HOW DO YOU LISTEN TO OTHERS?

What does it mean to listen with an open heart?
How do you like to be listened to?

Initial **thoughts & feelings** / One minute **rant**

I wonder and question...

What can we **carry forward** from the past?
What can we **leave behind?**

How do our **great-great-grandchildren**
hope we answer this question?

I wonder what the **dominant culture** is telling me?

What is the part of this **I don't want to talk about?**
What are the stories I am telling myself?

What does your **heart** want?

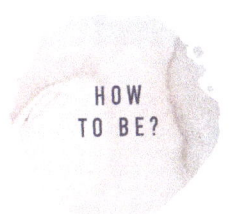  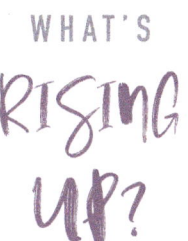  

This week, I intend to:

Four Windows of Wonder

THINKING · FEELING · SENSING · IMAGINING

How and what we *know*, and our definition of what it means *to know*, is limited.

When we expand our capacity to see in new ways, we become creative game changers and multi-dimensional problem solvers. We become more inclusive, more effective, and ultimately more capable of **creating a world that works for all.**

In many western cultures, *to know* comes from the thinking mind. From data, facts, calculations, rigorous scientific studies. And yet we have a heart-mind, we have a gut-brain, we have an imagination, and we have a sensing/feeling body. These are all ways of *knowing,* many of which have been diminished and even oppressed.

To limit our way of knowing to only *thinking* **shrinks our capacity to embody our wholeness, to be fully human.**

On the flip side, to embrace these other ways of knowing, to open ourselves up to relearning how to feel, sense and imagine, is to invite our whole selves to the table.

WHAT SENSATIONS DO YOU NOTICE IN YOUR BODY?

Achy	Prickly	Clammy	Tight	Slow
Numb	Stiff	Relaxed	Contained	Vibrating
Empty	Bruised	Tender	Open	Dull
Full	Pulsing	Clenched	Jumpy	Smooth
Cramped	Flowy	Releasing	Settled	Warm
Spacey	Still	Tense	Tingling	Electric
Airy	Burning	Cold	Contracted	Soft
Pain	Wiggly	Hot	Shaky	Wobbly
Spacious	Queasy	Rigid	Trembly	Sore
Blocked	Suffocated	Throbbing	Dizzy	Wooden
Pounding	Buzzy	Constricted	Shivery	Swirly
Sparkly	Radiating	Sensitive	Twitchy	
Breathless	Sweaty	Ripply	Drained	

> *Imagination is more important than knowledge. Knowledge is limited. Imagination encircles the world.*
> — ALBERT EINSTEIN

HOW ARE YOU *FEELING?*

SCARED
Frightened
Worried
Apprehensive
Panicky
Overwhelmed

FRUSTRATED
Anxious
Disturbed
Dismayed
Disappointed
Disheartened
Restless

GRIEF
Sadness
Depressed
Despair
Downtrodden
Hopeless
Regretful
Torn

CONCERNED
Overwhelmed
Confused
Shocked
Stunned
Appalled

ANGRY
Aggravated
Agitated
Annoyed
Impatient

PAIN
Agony
Hurt
Lonely
Isolated
Detached
Bored
Unwilling

STRESSED
Overwhelmed
Tired
Unclear
Foggy
Confused
Exhausted
Numb
Disconnected
Troubled
Fatigued
Burned-out
Embarrassed
Uncomfortable
Uneasy
Discomfort
Discombobulated

PEACEFUL
Ease
Serene
Tranquil
Calm
Relaxed

GRATEFUL
Thankful
Appreciative
Wowed

TENDER
Affectionate
Touched
Moved
Nurturing
Whimsical

EXCITED
Exuberant
Thrilled
Overjoyed
Amazed
Ecstatic
Enthusiastic
Ebullient
Energetic
Passionate

CURIOUS
Open
Engaged
Present
Resilient

HOPEFUL
Secure
Safe
Reassured

RELAXED
Chill
Rejuvenated
Light
Rested
Renewed
Comfortable

ATTENTIVE
Focused
Present
Engaged
Alert
Clear-headed

PLAYFUL
Joyful
Light
Empowered
Robust
Amused

HEALTHY
Well
Energetic
Fluid
Flowing
Alert
Alive
Lively

Facilitation Guide — INGREDIENTS FOR GROUPS

1. TIME DEMOCRACY

We live in a world with an imbalance in who gets to speak and be heard.

There are a multitude of reasons for this. It's both subtle and obvious. People with status and power often get more air time.

In our gatherings, we give everyone the same amount of time to be heard. If you don't want to speak, we will honor your time with silence.

We use a timer.

2. SILENT LISTENING

Most of us have been conditioned to listen and respond. Here, we listen in silence.

This allows us to deepen our understanding of the speaker and also to sit with our own thoughts, feelings and sensations. We notice what comes up without responding. We are enhancing our awareness of self and other, through silence.

We are practicing not advising, fixing, or consoling others.

5. DEEP CONFIDENTIALITY

Lessons can leave, personal stories must stay in the room.

Each person is welcome to share their own stories, but not the stories of *other participants*.

3. CULTIVATE WONDER

Judgments rise up for most of us when we hear other people's stories or thoughts.

We don't deny them, we simply move towards wonder. *I wonder why I think that? I wonder what that means to them?*

Wonder is a doorway to inclusivity.

4. TELL YOUR OWN STORY

We are practicing understanding and hearing differences.

We are speaking from the "I".
We are framing our stories as our own.
Our thoughts, our feelings, our beliefs.
Beliefs are different than truth.

We are developing discernment.

Our Process FOR GROUPS

Connect with us on our website if you have questions about how to use this process!

This process is approximately an hour long with a group of six people.

If your group is greater than six people, you will need to add more time to the two "Big Group Shares." We suggest choosing one question per session. This process works well on video conferencing platforms for groups who are geographically dispersed. The estimated times below are **based on a group of six.**

3 MIN — **Open your gathering with a pause** of some kind, an indication you are shifting out of normal socializing rules. Ideas might be three slow deep breaths, a short guided meditation, a minute of silence, reading a poem or piece of prose.

1 MIN — **Share names and pronouns** with one another.

3 MIN — **Recite the "ingredients"** from the facilitation guide, share why you are offering this gathering, and what excites or inspires you about *Wonder upRising.* Then share how the rest of gathering will flow.

12-15 MIN — Before you begin exploring the question, remind the group to wait to fill out the *"What's Rising Up?"* section until after the Big Group Share.

Begin with reading the question aloud. Set a timer for 10-12 minutes. During this time, people will write, draw, muse and contemplate the question and prompts.

12-15 MIN — First Round: Partner Share. Have people pair up. Each person in the pairing will have 2 or 3 minutes to share what came up in their writing/musing time with their partner. **Remind the group that this isn't a conversation, it's a listening practice.** One partner shares while the other is listening in silence. Have the pairs choose which partner will share first, set the timer and go. Repeat for the second person in the pair to share.

12 MIN — Second Round: Big Group Share. Go around the circle and have everyone share for 2 minutes with the larger group. Offer an optional 1 minute round for participants to reflect on what came up if there is time and interest. *(If the group is larger than 12, break into 2 smaller (big) groups of 6-12.)*

2 MIN — What's Rising Up? Now go back to the workbook and have everyone take 2 minutes to fill out the *"What's Rising Up?"* box.

6 MIN — Final Round: Big Group Share. One minute for each person to share **what rose up** for them and their intention for next week.

3 MIN — Closing Ritual. Create a ritual to close and seal your time together. Ideas might be: one minute of silence, standing and holding hands, three deep breaths, eye contact all around. Any practice that supports closing and grounding is welcome here.

? MIN — Social Time. If you want a little social time, leave space or add time for that. We've found that people enjoy connecting with each other after participating in this experience together!

FEELINGS ALLOWED AND EXPOSED,
SET US FREE.

BODIES LISTENED TO,
HEAL.

CREATIVITY REVEALS MAGIC,
CONNECTIVITY.

WRITTEN BY HAND.
SPOKEN BY MOUTH.
HEARD BY EARS.

CHANGE IS A GIVEN.
ENGAGEMENT IS A CHOICE.
EACH OF US PLAYS A PART.

CHOOSE YOURS.

© 2020 CAROL DELMONICO All rights reserved.